D1710202

High-flying Airplanes

Reagan Miller

🌲 Crabtree Publishing Company

www.crabtreebooks.com

Created by Bobbie Kalman

Author
Reagan Miller

Editorial director
Kathy Middleton

Project editor
Paul Challen

Editor
Adrianna Morganelli

Proofreaders
Rachel Stuckey
Crystal Sikkens

Photo research
Melissa McCLellan

Design
Tibor Choleva

Production coordinators
Katherine Berti
Margaret Amy Salter

Prepress technicians
Katherine Berti
Margaret Amy Salter

Consultant
Steve Taylor, Airline Captain

Illustrations
All illustrations by Leif Peng

Photographs
Dreamstime.com: © Rui Matos (page 4); © Ivan Cholakov (pages 6–7, 10 bottom, 11 bottom, 14); © Jvdwolf (page 16 top, 17 top); © Tom Dowd (page 18); © Lorpic99 (page 19); © Kelly Shaughnessy (page 20 inset); © Dmitry Skutin (page 21 inset);© Richard Cheesmar (page 22); © Orientaly 923 top); © Torben Meldgaard Madsen (page 23 bottom); © Jeffrey Banke (25 top); © Anthonyata (page 25 bottom); © James Bushelle (27 bottom)
Shutterstock.com: © Wojciech Beczynski (front cover); © ifong (title page); Ilja Mašík (table of contents page); © Rudchenko Liliia (blue sky–top pages); © Ivan Cholakov Gostock-dot-net (page 5 top); © Johnny Lye (page 8); © devi (page 8 inset); © Steve Collender (page 9 top); © Carlos E. Santa Maria (page 9 bottom); © Thor Jorgen Udvang (page 10 top); © haak78 (11 top); © Peter Guess (12 top); © DenisKlimov (page 13); © Ilja Mašík (page 15 top); © Jordan Tan (pages 16–17); © Yuriy Mykhaylov (pages 20–21); © Denton Rumsey (back cover, page 24); © Eugene Berman (page 26); © Konstantin L (27 top); © Dan Simonsen (28 top); © Merrill Dyck (page 28 bottom); © Chris Harvey (page 29); © Goran Bogicevi (page 31)
istockphoto: © sjlocke (page 12 bottom); © telegraham (17 top); © Andyworks (page 30)
NASA: page 15
Public Domain: page 5 bottom

Library and Archives Canada Cataloguing in Publication

Miller, Reagan
    High-flying airplanes / Reagan Miller.

(Vehicles on the move)
Includes index.
Issued also in an electronic format.
ISBN 978-0-7787-3047-7 (bound).--ISBN 978-0-7787-3061-3 (pbk.)

    1. Airplanes--Juvenile literature. I. Title. II. Series: Vehicles on the move

TL547.M54 2011   j629.133'34   C2010-904802-4

Library of Congress Cataloging-in-Publication Data

CIP available at Library of Congress

Crabtree Publishing Company

www.crabtreebooks.com   1-800-387-7650

Printed in the U.S.A./082010/BA20100709

Copyright © **2011 CRABTREE PUBLISHING COMPANY.** All rights reserved. No part of this publication may be reproduced, stored in a retrieval system or be transmitted in any form or by any means, electronic, mechanical, photocopying, recording, or otherwise, without the prior written permission of Crabtree Publishing Company. In Canada: We acknowledge the financial support of the Government of Canada through the Canada Book Fund for our publishing activities.

Published in Canada
Crabtree Publishing
616 Welland Ave.
St. Catharines, ON
L2M 5V6

Published in the United States
Crabtree Publishing
PMB 59051
350 Fifth Avenue, 59th Floor
New York, New York 10118

Published in the United Kingdom
Crabtree Publishing
Maritime House
Basin Road North, Hove
BN41 1WR

Published in Australia
Crabtree Publishing
386 Mt. Alexander Rd.
Ascot Vale (Melbourne)
VIC 3032

Contents

What is an airplane?

Airplanes are **vehicles**. Vehicles are machines that move people and things from place to place. There are different kinds of vehicles. Some travel on land, such as cars and trains. Others travel on water, such as boats. Airplanes travel in the air. Airplanes travel faster than any other vehicle.

*This airplane is a **passenger plane**. Passenger planes are built to move people long distances. Have you ever seen a passenger plane flying in the sky?*

Off to a flying start!

In 1903, Orville and Wilbur Wright became the first people to fly a powered airplane. Their first flight lasted only a few seconds. Since that time, airplanes have changed a lot.

This is the first flight of the Wright Flyer I, with Orville piloting and Wilbur running at wingtip.

Plane parts

Airplanes have many parts. Each part does a different job. Almost all airplanes have the same main parts. Look at the picture below to learn more!

Tail: *The tail is at the back of the plane. The tail helps guide the plane in the air. It also helps the plane turn.*

Wing: *The wing comes out of the side of the fuselage. The wing is flat on the bottom and has a small curve on the top. The wing's shape helps lift the airplane up in the air.*

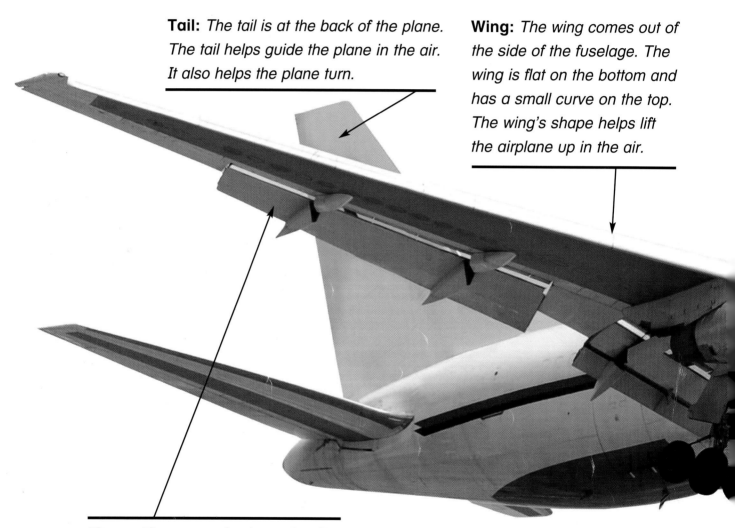

Flaps: *Flaps are raised on takeoff to help create lift. When flaps are lowered, they act as brakes, slowing the plan down during landings.*

There are many different kinds of planes. Different planes are built to do different jobs. Some planes are built to fly people over long distances. Other planes are built to do tricks or stunts. There are even planes that help put out wildfires. Keep reading to learn more about amazing airplanes!

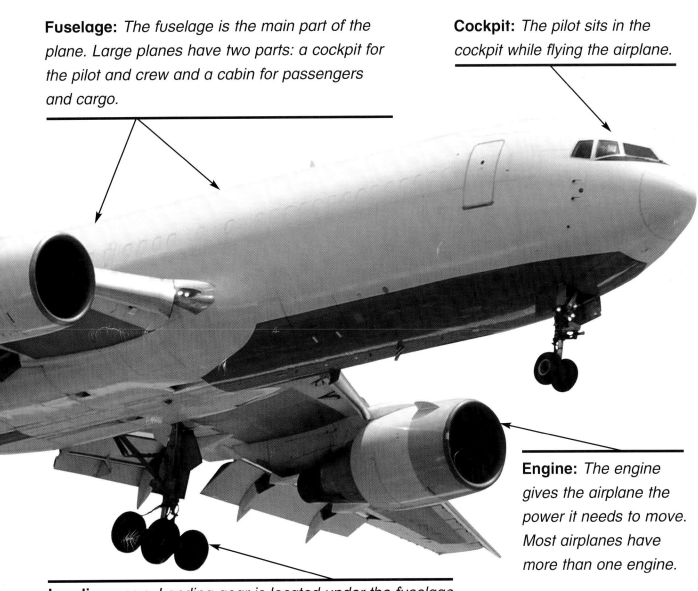

Fuselage: *The fuselage is the main part of the plane. Large planes have two parts: a cockpit for the pilot and crew and a cabin for passengers and cargo.*

Cockpit: *The pilot sits in the cockpit while flying the airplane.*

Engine: *The engine gives the airplane the power it needs to move. Most airplanes have more than one engine.*

Landing gear: *Landing gear is located under the fuselage. The wheels help airplanes gather speed as they take off and slow to a stop as they land.*

Ready for the runway!

An airport is a place where airplanes arrive and depart. Airports have runways. Runways are long strips of pavement that airplanes use to take off and land.

runways

airport

The wheels lift up inside the plane after it takes off. They come down again when the plane is preparing to land.

wheels

Cockpit controls

The pilot controls the plane from the cockpit. The pilot uses a control stick to fly the plane. The pilot moves the control stick forward, backward, and sideways to control the direction of the plane.

Small airplanes have cockpits, too. Pilots use the cockpit controls to guide a plane on the ground and in the air.

control stick

There are many computer screens inside a cockpit. The screens show how high and how quickly the plane is flying. There is always a pilot and a copilot to fly large planes.

9

Start your engines!

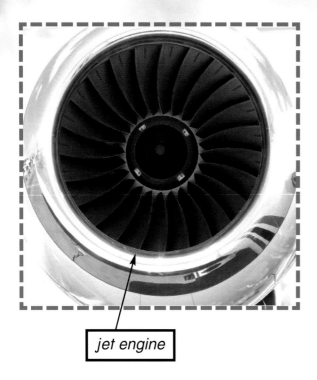

jet engine

The fastest airplanes have **jet engines**. Jet engines suck in air through the front of the engine. The air is mixed with fuel and then forced out the back of the engine. This force moves the airplane forward.

jet engines

Taking a spin

Some airplanes have **propellers**. The engines make the propellers spin around quickly on the front of the airplane. The propellers pull the airplane through the air.

propeller

propellers

Come fly with me!

Look up in the sky. There is a good chance you will see a passenger plane fly by. Passenger planes, or airliners, are the most common planes. These planes are used to carry passengers to places all over the world. Each day, thousands of passenger planes take flight all over the world.

Flight attendants are members of the airline crew who ensure the safety and comfort of passengers.

Big and small

The largest passenger planes are called **jumbo jets**. Some jumbo jets can carry more than 500 passengers! Jumbo jets are used to travel long distances.

Some passenger planes are small. These planes carry fewer passengers than jumbo jets. Small passenger planes are used to travel shorter distances.

An Airbus A380 is the world's largest passenger plane. It can carry up to 853 passengers.

Cargo planes

Cargo planes are used to carry cargo instead of passengers. Cargo is products that are moved in vehicles such as ships, trucks, or airplanes.

Cargo planes are used to move things from place to place quickly. A cargo plane may be used to carry things such as mail, fresh flowers, and foods. Some cargo planes deliver supplies, food, water, and blankets to places after earthquakes, big storms, and other emergencies.

The largest cargo plane is the Antonov AN-225. Its cargo hold is large enough to carry 80 cars! This plane is delivering supplies to Haiti after an earthquake.

Carrying the load

Most of the space inside a cargo plane is for carrying cargo. Cargo is held in a cargo hold. Cargo planes have large doors that open wide so cargo can be loaded easily. Some cargo planes have openings on the nose, or front tip, of the plane. The nose can be flipped open to load and unload large cargo.

A Super Transporter is a cargo plane that is used to move really large cargo. These planes can carry large items such as military tanks and even helicopters!

Military planes

Military planes are used by people in the military. There are different kinds of military planes built to do different jobs.

Transport airplanes are used to carry soldiers and supplies to the places they are needed.

Hercules transport plane

An RQ-4 Global Hawk spy plane

A **bomber plane** is larger and slower than a fighter plane. A bomber plane carries bombs and drops them onto places on the ground.

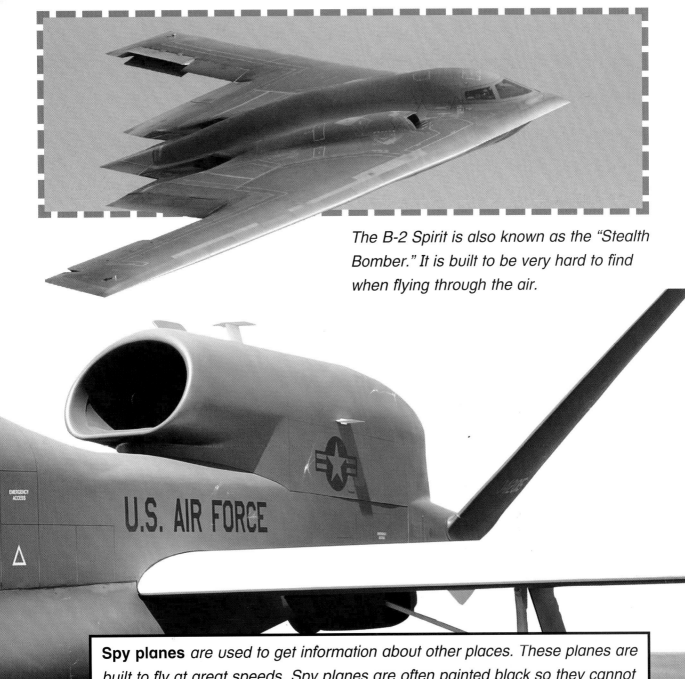

The B-2 Spirit is also known as the "Stealth Bomber." It is built to be very hard to find when flying through the air.

U.S. AIR FORCE

Spy planes are used to get information about other places. These planes are built to fly at great speeds. Spy planes are often painted black so they cannot be seen at night. An RQ-4 Global Hawk can be controlled without a pilot on board. It can fly over 40,000 square miles (103,600 km²) a day.

Fighter planes

Fighter planes are small, fast-moving planes that are used to attack enemy planes in the sky. They are equipped with weapons and are designed so that it is difficult for enemy planes to find them. Fighter pilots need many hours of practice to be able to operate these planes.

one-pilot cockpit

The Lockheed Martin/Boeing F-22 Raptor is a very fast fighter airplane. It is not easy for enemy planes to see it in the air.

Fill it up!

Fighter planes are built to be small and fast. They cannot hold a lot of fuel. Some fighter planes can refuel while still in the air. **Refueling planes** are special planes that are built to fly close to a fighter plane to fill up its fuel tank.

refueling plane

tube

fighter jet

The refueling plane has a long tube that connects to the fuel tank of the fighter plane. The refueling plane pumps fuel through the tube into the fighter plane. The fighter plane can then continue to fly without having to land to get more fuel.

Making a splash

Floatplanes are built to take off and land in water. Floatplanes have floats instead of wheels. Instead of using a runway, these planes gain speed for takeoff by moving through the water like a boat.

floats

Floatplanes are useful when flying to small islands that do not have runways on which regular planes can land.

A plane for all seasons

Some floatplanes have skis instead of floats. These planes are used to land in places covered by snow and ice.

skis

Planes with skis can land in remote northern locations where the ground is frozen or covered with snow.

Firefighting planes

Firefighting planes are used for putting out forest fires. A firefighting plane has a large tank in the fuselage that can be filled with water. The plane fills up the tank by skimming across the water of lakes, big rivers, or seas.

This firefighting plane is the Canadair CL-215 Scooper. It can scoop water into its tank and drop the load on forest fires.

Putting out the fire

When the tank is full, the plane flies above a fire and dumps the water from the tank onto the flames below.

(above) A Canadair CL-215 Scooper firefighting airplane drops water on a forest fire.

Airplanes can also carry and drop fire retardants. Fire retardants help delay or prevent a fire from spreading. They are often colored red to mark where they have been dropped.

Agricultural planes

Crop dusters are planes that are used to spray crops. These planes are flown over fields. The plane sprays a chemical mixture on the crops to protect them from insects. They can also spray fertilizer to help the plants grow.

crop-duster airplane

spray mixture

crops

Crop-duster airplanes fly low to the ground to stop the sprayed materials from drifting away. They often fly only 15 feet (4.6 m) above ground.

Look out below

Crop dusters have to fly low to the ground to make sure that what they are spraying makes it to the ground. These planes often have to fly around trees or below electrical wires.

It is not unusual for crop-duster pilots to fly under power or telephone lines.

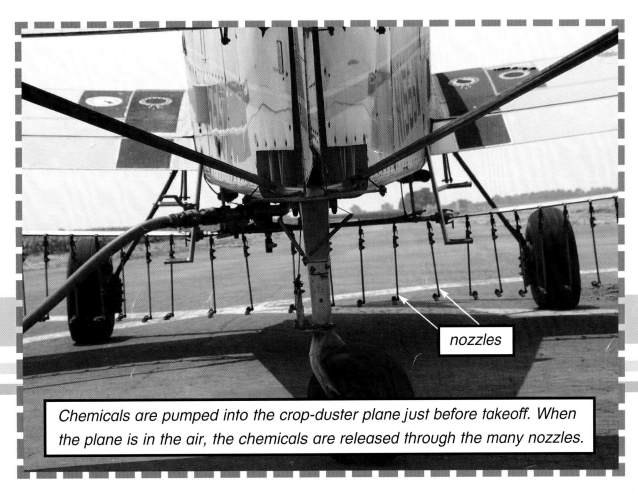

nozzles

Chemicals are pumped into the crop-duster plane just before takeoff. When the plane is in the air, the chemicals are released through the many nozzles.

Fancy flying

Stunt planes are planes that are built to perform at air shows. These planes perform tricks in the air. Stunt planes are often small so they can move easily through the air. They can be jet powered or propeller driven.

Stunt planes perform many tricks. This stunt plane just landed on top of a pickup truck.

Tricky operators

Stunt pilots are specially trained
to perform difficult moves such as
loops, rolls, and spins. These moves
are called "aerobatics."

This biplane is doing a loop at an air show. Biplanes have two wings.

Nice form!

A group of stunt planes is called a **squadron**. At an air show, a squadron flies close together to make a formation. A formation is a shape such as a diamond or a square.

Stunt pilots have to practice a lot to perform formations safely and correctly.

The Snowbirds demonstration team performs a diamond formation in jet-powered planes. The pilots work as a team to bring interesting performances to air shows.

With flying colors!

Some stunt planes are built to release colorful smoke trails as they perform tricks and formations. The smoke makes colorful designs in the sky.

The smoke helps the crowd follow the path of the fast-moving planes.

More flying fun!

Gliders are planes that do not have engines. A glider cannot take off on its own. It is often attached to an engine-powered airplane with a cable. The airplane helps launch the glider into the air. Once the glider is in the air, the cable is removed and the glider can fly through the air on its own.

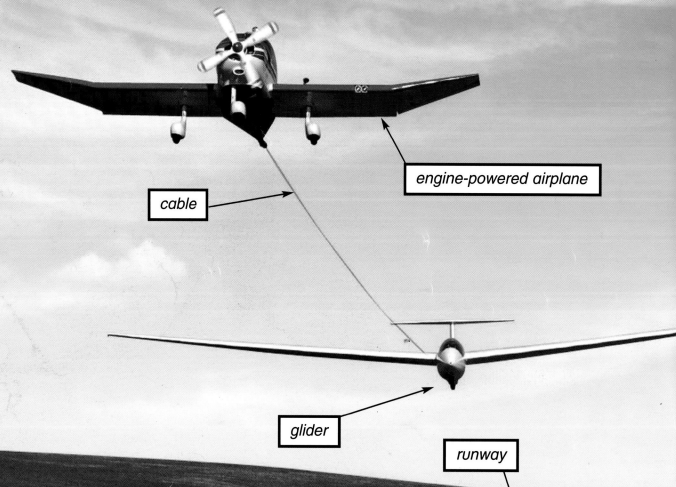

cable

engine-powered airplane

glider

runway

Ultralights

An **ultralight** is a very small airplane. It has a small engine and a propeller. Most ultralights can fit only one person.

Ultralight planes come in many different shapes and designs.

Words to know and Index

cargo planes
pages 14–15

crop-duster planes
pages 24–25

firefighting planes
pages 22–23

fighter planes
pages 18–19

gliders
page 30

floatplanes
pages 20–21

passenger planes
pages 4, 12–13

stunt planes
pages 26–29

Other index words
airplanes 4
jet engines 10, 26
military planes 16
propellers 11, 26, 31

ultralight planes
page 31